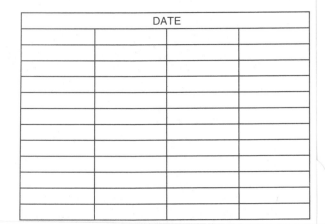

DATE			

Artisans Around the World

Africa South of the Sahara

Susan Rich, Margot Volem, and Cynthia A. Black

RSVP®

**RAINTREE
STECK-VAUGHN**
P U B L I S H E R S
A Steck-Vaughn Company

Austin, Texas

www.steck-vaughn.com

Developed by Franklin Tull, Inc.,
Manager: Sharon Franklin
Designer: Dahna Solar
Maps: Terragraphics, Inc.
Illustrators: Dahna Solar and James Cloutier
Picture Researcher: Mary Tull
Projects: Cynthia A. Black

Raintree Steck-Vaughn Publishers Staff
Project Manager: Joyce Spicer
Editor: Pam Wells
Electronic Production: Scott Melcer

Photo Credits: Carl Purcell/The Stock Solution: p. 8UR; CORBIS/Patrick Bennett: p. 8LL; CHOICE Humanitarian:
pp. 8UL, 8LL; Graeme Milton/The Stock Solution: p. 9UR; James Cloutier: pp. 11UR, 11LR, 30L; Ken Cole/The Stock
Solution: pp. 12UR, 12LL; Matthew Krabill: pp. 16LL, 16LR, 18UR, 19UL, 22CR; CORBIS/Chase Swift: p. 16UL;
CORBIS/Hulton-Deutsch Collection: p. 17LL; CORBIS/ Werner Forman: p. 20UR; CORBIS/Peter Johnson: pp. 21UL, 21LL,
26UR; Jean Higgins/Unicorn Stock Photos: pp. 26LR, 29UL, 30UR; South African Tourism Board: pp. 26UL, 26LL, 28UL;
CORBIS/Anthony Bannister: p. 27UR; CORBIS/Charles O'Rear: p. 27LL; CORBIS/Peter Turnley: p. 38UR; A.
Ramey/Unicorn Stock Photos: p. 29UR; CORBIS/Paul Almasy: p. 34LL; CORBIS/Carmen Redondo: p. 34UR; Robert
Maust/Photo Agora: pp. 34LR, 35LL, 36UR; Stan Osolinski/The Stock Solution: p. 37CR; CORBIS/Otto Lang: p. 38LR;
CORBIS/Studio Patellani: p. 40UR; CORBIS/Charles & Josette Lenars: p. 40LL. All project photos by
James Cloutier.
[**Photo credit key:** First Letter: U-Upper; C-Center, L-Lower; Second letter: R-Right; L-Left]

Library of Congress Cataloging-in-Publication Data
Rich, Susan, 1959-
    Africa south of the Sahara / Susan Rich, Margot Volem, and Cynthia A. Black.
        p.   cm. — (Artisans around the world)
    Includes bibliographical references and index.
    Summary: Presents brief historical information and instructions for craft projects representative of the people of
Kenya, Benin, South Africa, and Congo.
    ISBN 0-7398-0118-X
    1. Material culture — Africa, Sub-Saharan Juvenile literature. 2. Folk art — Africa, Sub-Saharan Juvenile literature.
3. Ethnic art — Africa, Sub-Saharan Juvenile literature. 4. Artisans — Africa, Sub-Saharan Juvenile literature. 5. Africa,
Sub-Saharan — Social life and customs Juvenile literature. 6. Creative activities and seat work Juvenile literature.
I. Volem, Margot. II. Black, Cynthia A. III. Title. IV. Series.
GN645.R53   1999
306'.0967—dc21   99-21171
                                                                                                        CIP   AC

Printed and bound in the United States
1 2 3 4 5 6 7 8 9 0 WO 03 02 01 00 99

Table of Contents

The icons next to the projects in the Table of Contents identify the easiest and the most challenging project in the book. This may help you decide which project to do first.

⇨ easiest project

✪ most challenging project

Benin

Congo

Kenya

South
Africa

Africa South of
the Sahara

N
W E
S

0   800 miles
0   1200 km

Introduction to Artisans Around the World

There are many ways to learn about the history and present-day life of people in other countries. In school, students often study the history of a country to learn about its people. In this series, you will learn about the history, geography, and the way of life of groups of people through their folk art. People who create folk art are called **artisans.** They are skilled in an art, a craft, or a trade. You will then have a chance to create your own folk art, using your own ideas and symbols.

What Is Folk Art?

Folk art is not considered "fine art." Unlike many fine artists, folk artisans do not generally go to school to learn how to do their art. Very few folk artists are known as "famous" outside of their countries or even their towns. Folk art is the art of everyday people of a region. In this series, folk art also includes primitive art, that is, the art of the first people to be in an area. But, beware! Do not let this fool you into thinking that folk art is not "real" art. As you will see, the quality of the folk art in this series is amazing by any standards.

Folk art comes from the heart and soul of common people. It is an expression of their feelings. Often, it shows their personal, political, or religious beliefs. It may also have a practical purpose or meet a specific need, such as the need for shelter. In many cases, the folk art in the "Artisans Around the World" series comes from groups of people who did not even have a word for art in their culture. Art was simply what people did. It was a part of being human.

Introduction to *Africa South of the Sahara*

In this book, you will learn about these crafts and the people who do them:

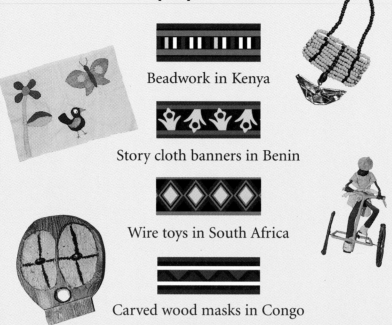

Beadwork in Kenya

Story cloth banners in Benin

Wire toys in South Africa

Carved wood masks in Congo

Then you will learn how to do projects of your own.

Here are some questions to think about as you read this book:

Did any of these folk arts help to meet specific needs?
If so, in what way?

Which folk arts expressed people's religious, political, or personal views?

Were some of these folk arts traditionally created mostly by men or by women?
Why do you think that was so? Is it still true today?

How did the history of a country influence some folk art traditions?

How did the geography, including the natural resources, of a country
influence some folk art traditions? How did people get folk art materials
that they needed but that were not found in their region?

Do some folk art traditions tell a story about a group of people or a culture?
If so, in what way?

How have these folk art traditions been passed down from generation to generation?

Folk Art Today

Reading about these folk art traditions, as well as creating your own folk art,
will increase your respect for the people who first did them.
Do you think some of these art forms, such as story cloth banners,
could be created faster or more easily using machines,
like the sewing machine, or technology, like the computer?
Do you think anything would be lost by doing so, even if it were possible?

All of these folk art traditions of Africa south of the Sahara began long ago.
Can you think of any new folk art traditions being started now, in the
United States or in other countries? If so, what are they?
If not, why do you think there are no new traditions?

Safety Guidelines

These folk art projects are a lot of fun to do. But it's important to follow basic safety rules as you work. Here are some guidelines to follow as you complete the projects in this book. Work slowly and carefully. That way you can enjoy the process.

1. Part of being a responsible person of any age is knowing when to ask for help. Some of these projects are challenging. Ask an adult for help whenever you need it. Even where the book does not tell you to, feel free to ask for help if you need it.

2. Handle all pointed tools, such as scissors, in a safe manner. Keep them stored in a safe place when not in use.

3. Wear gloves to protect your hands from sharp edges while cutting aluminum. Have an adult work with you.

4. Woodcarving Safety
   • Have an adult work with you when you are cutting and drilling.
   • Learn the correct way to use a tool, and use it for its intended purpose only.
   • Always clamp the wood to a firm base before carving. Protect the table with an old towel.
   • Use common sense! Never put your fingers in front of the chisel when you are carving. Cut away from yourself and others.
   • Ask an adult to sharpen your tools for you.

5. When painting, protect your clothing with an old shirt or a smock. When wet, acrylic paint can be removed with water. After it dries, it cannot be removed.

By the way, part of being an artist involves cleaning up! Be sure to clean up your work area when you are finished. Also, remember to thank anyone who helped you.

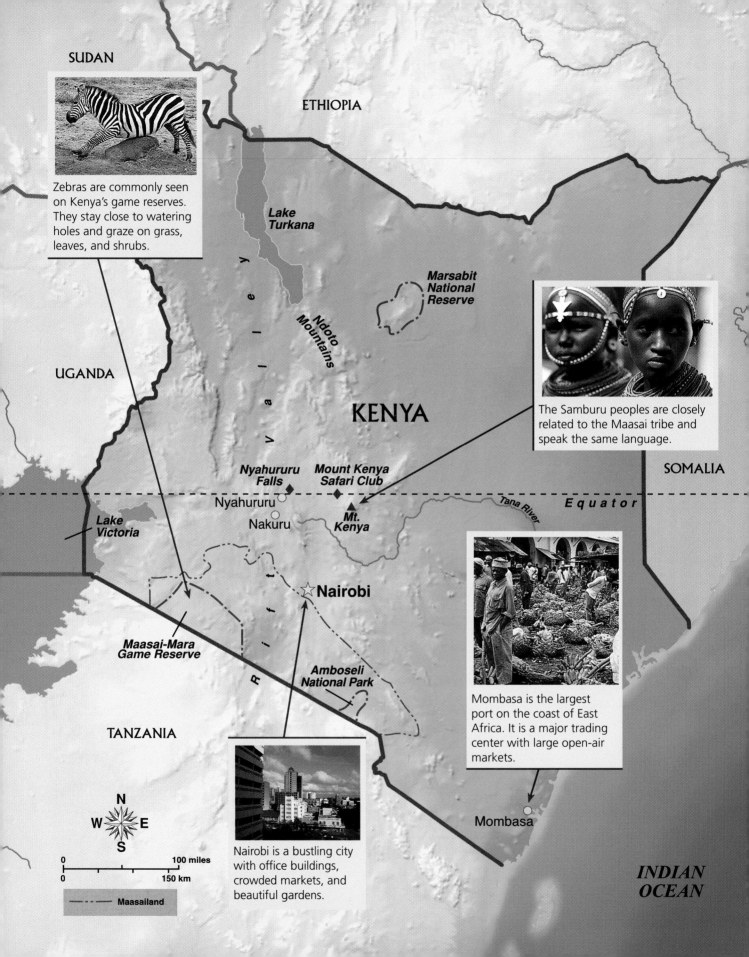

SUDAN

Zebras are commonly seen on Kenya's game reserves. They stay close to watering holes and graze on grass, leaves, and shrubs.

ETHIOPIA

Lake Turkana

Marsabit National Reserve

Ndoto Mountains

UGANDA

KENYA

The Samburu peoples are closely related to the Maasai tribe and speak the same language.

SOMALIA

Nyahururu Falls

Mount Kenya Safari Club

Nyahururu

Tana River

Equator

Nakuru

Mt. Kenya

Lake Victoria

Maasai-Mara Game Reserve

☆ **Nairobi**

Amboseli National Park

Mombasa is the largest port on the coast of East Africa. It is a major trading center with large open-air markets.

TANZANIA

N
W · E
S

0 ___ 100 miles
0 ___ 150 km

—··— Maasailand

Nairobi is a bustling city with office buildings, crowded markets, and beautiful gardens.

Mombasa

INDIAN OCEAN

Kenya

▲ Mount Kenya rises over 17,000 feet (5,199 m) in Kenya's Central Highlands.

Kenya Facts

Name: Kenya (Republic of Kenya)
Capital: Nairobi
Borders: Ethiopia, Sudan, Somalia, Indian Ocean, Uganda, and Tanzania
Population: 28,800,000; the Maasai number less than 250,000
Language: English, Swahili, and many other native, or original, languages
Size: 224,081 sq.mi. (580,369 sq km)
High/Low Points: Mount Kenya 17,058 ft. (5,199 m); sea level
Climate: The coast is hot and humid except in winter; inland, the days are warm and sunny with little humidity; temperatures average 80° F (27° C) in the lowlands and 60° F (16° C) at the highest levels
Wildlife: Perhaps the most plentiful in Africa, including lions, crocodiles, cheetahs, pink flamingos, elephants, leopards, gazelles, and rhinoceroses. Each September, millions of zebras and wildebeests move south across the Maasai-Mara Game Reserve.
Plants: Baobab and acacia trees grow on the plains, while evergreen forests cover the slopes of Mount Kenya. Higher up the mountain is the remarkable groundsel tree with cabbagelike flowers. Mangrove trees are found along the coast.

Tennis from North to South

In the 1940s a Hollywood movie star named William Holden built his own private clubhouse in Kenya. There he entertained famous actors, writers, and artists. Today the Mount Kenya Safari Club is open to everyone. The club's tennis courts have one unique feature. The net follows the exact line of the equator. As one player serves the ball in the southern **hemisphere**, the other player volleys from the northern hemisphere!

Journey to the Center of the Earth

Imagine drawing a line through the center of Kenya. If someone stepped on that line, he or she would be standing right on the equator. Kenya is a diverse country with tall mountains, lakes, and valleys. The northern and eastern regions are dry, scrub desert. The Central Highlands are the most fertile area of the country and home of Mount Kenya. The Rift Valley is dotted with **extinct** volcanoes. Poor drainage from these slopes results in the shallow waters of soda lakes. These lakes are home to millions of birds that flock there each year.

The Birthplace of Humanity

The Rift Valley is also known as the "Cradle of Humanity," as a result of the Leakey family's important **archaeological** and anthropological discoveries around Lake Turkana. There, in 1972, Dr. Richard Leakey found part of an early genus *Homo* skull, believed to be 1.9 million years old. This find, and others, changed scientists' ideas on the origin of human beings.

A Traveling People

The Rift Valley is home to a number of **nomadic** groups of people who move seasonally from place to place. One of these groups, the Maasai, probably migrated, or moved, from the Nile Valley of Egypt more than 400 years ago. Some people believe the Maasai originally came from Israel. By the early 1900s, Maasailand covered 77,000 square miles (199,430 sq km) in the central region of Kenya. British colonists soon acquired grazing land from the Maasai. After long talks with Maasai elders, treaties were drawn up that gave some of Maasailand to the British. But in return, the British agreed to leave the rest of Maasailand, and its lifestyle, in peace. This is why there are so few roads and other services, including electricity, in Maasailand today.

Maasai, a Highly Structured Society

Traditionally the Maasai are a nomadic people. Yet today many Maasai live year-round in villages and farming communities. The Maasai are divided into five clans, or groups, each located in a different geographic area. Each area has many homesteads, or communities, made up of several families. The boys from these families are grouped into "age-sets," or groups of boys their age. They are a part of this same group of boys, and later, men, for life.

The relationships between boys of the same age-set is as strong as the bond between brothers. For example, a Maasai warrior must never eat alone. Wealthy Maasai warriors always invite their poorer age-set friends to join them for meals. Wealthy Maasai families are expected to share their wealth with the rest of the community.

The Ways of a Warrior

In the past it was the warrior's job to protect his community from hungry lions and cattle raids by neighboring groups. Today he must still protect his people, but this usually means finding good grazing lands for the cattle or keeping the village secure. Cattle raids do not happen often. Also, the Kenyan government has outlawed lion hunting, which traditionally gave honor to the warrior. Still, the **rituals,** or ceremonies, that surround a boy's passage to becoming a warrior are an important part of Maasai life. This stage of young adulthood, or "warriorhood," is thought to be the best stage of a man's life.

Being a warrior is not just about killing lions. A respected warrior must be gentle as well as strong. He should enjoy hunting and poetry. At the age of 15, a boy learns to be a warrior by attending a feasting camp held far from the village. There the warriors learn to hunt, plan cattle raids, and explore the area. "Today hunting isn't a big thing," one Maasai warrior explained. "It is just to discipline the lions when they attack cows."

A Cattle-Centered Universe

A Maasai proverb says a man is not wealthy unless he has children and cattle. Cattle are very important to the Maasai. They provide meat, milk, and blood, which men drink for extra strength. Hides for housing, clothes, and blankets also come from cattle. Children are taught to recognize each cow's or bull's personality. The Maasai believe that in the beginning all the cattle on earth were given to them by *Enkai,* their god. In a recent census, or count, it was found that the Maasai own 3 million cattle. That is more cattle per person than any other people in Africa.

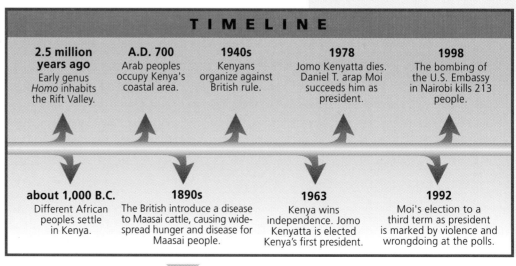

TIMELINE

2.5 million years ago
Early genus *Homo* inhabits the Rift Valley.

A.D. 700
Arab peoples occupy Kenya's coastal area.

1940s
Kenyans organize against British rule.

1978
Jomo Kenyatta dies. Daniel T. arap Moi succeeds him as president.

1998
The bombing of the U.S. Embassy in Nairobi kills 213 people.

about 1,000 B.C.
Different African peoples settle in Kenya.

1890s
The British introduce a disease to Maasai cattle, causing widespread hunger and disease for Maasai people.

1963
Kenya wins independence. Jomo Kenyatta is elected Kenya's first president.

1992
Moi's election to a third term as president is marked by violence and wrongdoing at the polls.

Maasai Girls

At about age 10, a Maasai girl is responsible for caring for her younger sisters and brothers. She also must learn what will be expected of her when she becomes a woman. Maasai women build their own houses from branches and grass. A layer of cow manure provides insulation, or protection from the weather. Women are considered the heads of the household. A man cannot enter his wife's home without her permission.

After the day's chores are completed, Maasai girls and women come together to bead necklaces, belts, and earrings. Women design the beaded jewelry that Maasai warriors wear for special ceremonies and for hunting. A man's girlfriend makes his ankle bracelets and upper armbands. They are considered important signs of love.

▲ Maasai women and girls work together to make colorful patterned jewelry out of beads.

The Language of Beads

Before Arab traders brought the first glass beads from China and Persia (now Iran), Maasai women made beads from bone, iron, and clay. Today, glass beads from the Czech Republic are the most popular and the most expensive. A Maasai family may sell cattle in order to buy beads.

In Maa, the Maasai language, there are over 40 words for different types of beadwork. The patterns in a necklace tell whether a woman is married, if she has a child, and whether she is the mother of a warrior. Each band of color has a secret meaning. Maasai women are very particular about which colors are placed together and when a piece of jewelry is worn. For example, a special necklace that reaches the knees is worn only by a bride on her wedding day. Some Maasai say that blue beads are god, because they are the color of the sky that god inhabits. Green stands for a lush landscape after a rainfall, a sign of peace. One popular color pattern—red, white, black, and green—represents the colors of the Kenyan flag.

Samburu Means "Butterfly"

The Maasai are not the only ones who love to wear beads. A Maasai neighbor, the Samburu, also wear colorful beads. The young girls receive beads as gifts from their admirers. At the age of 15, a girl should have collected enough beads to invite a proposal of marriage. This happens when necklaces cover her from shoulders to chin. Her chin must rest on top of a tower of beads.

Each band of color in ▶ Maasai beadwork has powerful secret meanings.

11

Maasai Decoration

Decorating the body is the Maasai's main art form. Beaded collars, skirts, and tiny boxes are the Maasai's artistic treasures. The objects worn change as a person moves through the stages of childhood, warriorhood, marriage, and finally becomes an elder.

A child's first strand of beads is tied around his or her waist to show that the toddler is loved. By age seven or eight, boys and girls get their ears pierced and begin wearing beaded earrings. By the age of 12, young girls have long swinging earrings and flat beaded collars designed to draw attention to their graceful movements. A warrior's belts and necklaces are signs of a woman's love. A married woman wears long beaded earrings that touch her shoulders. A married man does not need much jewelry. He wears a tiny beaded box, a gift from his oldest daughter.

Survival of the Maasai

Some Maasai worry that they are a people whose time has passed. Today it is becoming more difficult for the Maasai culture to survive. The loss of land continues, and without land there is no place for the cattle to graze. Without land, there is no place for the warriors to build their ceremonial camps. And without cattle and ceremonies, the Maasai culture will disappear. However, the Maasai are learning to adapt to these changing conditions. Many Maasai warriors today understand the need for education. They are studying to become doctors, lawyers, and teachers in order to help ensure their people's survival.

▲ In Maasai culture, men decorate their bodies with beaded earrings, necklaces, and other items.

◄ The Maasai village community struggles to keep their culture alive and practice their honored traditions.

Tools

- beading tray or shallow box
- long beading needle
- scissors
- needle-nosed and round-nosed pliers
- hammer and nail or awl

Materials

- seed beads and larger oval beads
- fine beading wire
- strong cotton beading thread or carpet thread
- aluminum pie pan
- scraps of leather
- wire earring hooks
- white glue

Maasai Beadwork Hints

- Light colors like yellow or white are usually separated by darker or brighter colors.

- A repeating pattern of black and white, black and red, and black and yellow beads is common.

- Most beadwork has stripes or wide bands of contrasting colors.

- Maasai patterns are rarely **symmetrical,** or balanced. Repeated bands of color are often uneven in width.

Make colorful beaded ornaments, necklaces, and armbands in the style of the Maasai.

Prepare to Bead

1. Make a plan for your finished project. Get ideas from the bold colors and patterns of Maasai beadwork. Read the hints on this page.

2. Pour out the beads you will use, a little at a time. Separate your beads in a beading tray or on a towel in a shallow box.

3. Collect the other materials you will need. Test the wire or needle to see if it fits through the beads. Always use the thickest thread or wire possible so that the beads won't slide up and down.

Beaded Ornaments

The Maasai use colorful beaded ornaments as earrings or to hang on necklaces.

1. Practice bending and twisting the wire into shapes using needle-nosed pliers. Use the round-nosed pliers to make wire loops. *(See diagram.)*

2. To make a square ornament, form a wire frame. String beads loosely around the frame. Working from the bottom up, add rows of beads on short wires to fill the inside of the frame. Loop the wires between the beads already on the frame. (If the frame is too tight for a wire to fit, break off a bead. Hold the ornament under the table and squeeze one bead with pliers.) *(See diagram.)*

3. To make a round ornament, string six beads on a piece of wire. Bend the wire into a small circle, and twist closed with the pliers. String the second row of beads, and bend these around the first. Twist closed and cut the wire, leaving a short end for a loop to hang the ornament. *(See diagram.)*

Beaded Ornaments

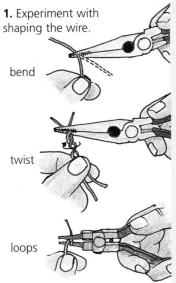

1. Experiment with shaping the wire.

bend

twist

loops

2. Make a square ornament.

frame   close up

3. Make a round ornament.

▲ Get together with your friends to experiment with beading.

4. The Maasai also make shiny aluminum ornaments. Use an old pair of scissors to cut a section out of an old aluminum pie pan. **Wear gloves to protect your hands from the sharp edges**. **Have an adult work with you on the cutting.** Cut out small triangles or circles. Carefully fold the edges over, and squeeze them flat with pliers. Poke a hole in the top of each ornament with a needle. *(See diagram.)*

5. Use a loop of wire or thread to attach the ornament to an earring hook or to a necklace. *(See diagram.)*

Strands of Beads

The Maasai wear strands of beads around the wrist, neck, and across the chest. The strands often have ornaments dangling from them.

1. Plan the order in which you will string the beads. You can use the groove in the beading tray. You can also fold a piece of thin cardboard into a W, and place the beads in order in the creases. *(See diagram.)*

2. Decide how long the strand will be. It should be at least long enough to slide over your head. For a wrist band, measure around the wide part of your hand. Cut a piece of thread twice the finished length, plus 12 inches (30 cm). Thread the needle, and double the thread over. Tie one bead onto the end of the doubled thread to act as a stopper. *(See diagram.)*

3. If you want, connect two or more strands of beads with leather spacers. To make spacers, cut small circles or strips of thin leather. Poke holes with an awl, or use a hammer and nail. *(See diagram.)*

4. String the beads to the length you planned, adding ornaments and spacers as you go. *(See diagram.)*

5. To finish, tie the ends of the thread together with a square knot. Slide the knot as close to the beads as possible, and pull it very tight. Cut off the needle and the stopper bead. Put a dot of glue on the knot. Slide the thread ends in under the beads. *(See diagram.)*

4. Make aluminum ornament.

5. Attach the ornament.

Strands of Beads

1. Plan the stringing order.

2. Cut a thread.

stopper bead

3. Make spacers.

4. Add ornaments and spacers.

5. Tie a square knot.

14

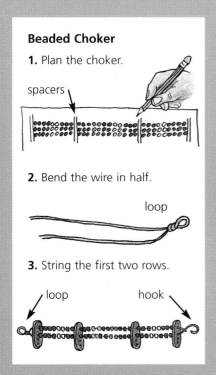

Beaded Arm Bands

1. Form the leather ring.

2. Wrap beads around the ring.

stitch

Beaded Choker

1. Plan the choker.

spacers

2. Bend the wire in half.

loop

3. String the first two rows.

loop   hook

Beaded Arm Bands

The Maasai often string beads around a strip of leather or rubber. These are worn around the wrists, arms, and ankles.

1. Cut a strip of leather to any width. Form it into a ring big enough to slide over your hand or foot. Stitch the edges of the leather together. Use pliers to pull the needle through the leather, or poke holes with an awl or with a hammer and nail. *(See diagram.)*

2. Thread a beading needle with a long piece of thread, and knot it. Take a small stitch in the edge of the leather. String enough beads to wrap once around the ring. Pull the loop tight. Slip the needle over and then under the thread just above the first bead. Pull the stitch tight. Wrap more rows of beads around the ring. Make a stitch after each row. *(See diagram.)*

Beaded Choker

The Maasai make beautiful choker necklaces and wide collars by stringing rows of beads on wires that are connected with spacers.

1. Decide how many rows of beads you want to string. Plan the colors and patterns, so that they line up from row to row. It's common to use larger beads on the top and bottom rows. Decide how many spacers you will use (four or more) and how you will space them. *(See diagram.)*

2. Measure around your neck for the length of your choker. Cut a piece of beading wire long enough for two rows plus six inches (15 cm). Bend the wire in half and twist a small loop at the center. *(See diagram.)*

3. Make the spacers. Insert the ends of the wire into the top two holes of the first spacer and slide it to the loop. String the first two rows of beads. Add spacers as planned, and end with a spacer. Twist the wire ends closed. Form a hook out of the leftover wire. Repeat for the next rows of beads. On the bottom row, string ornaments if you want. *(See diagram.)*

Finished beadwork ▶ by students.

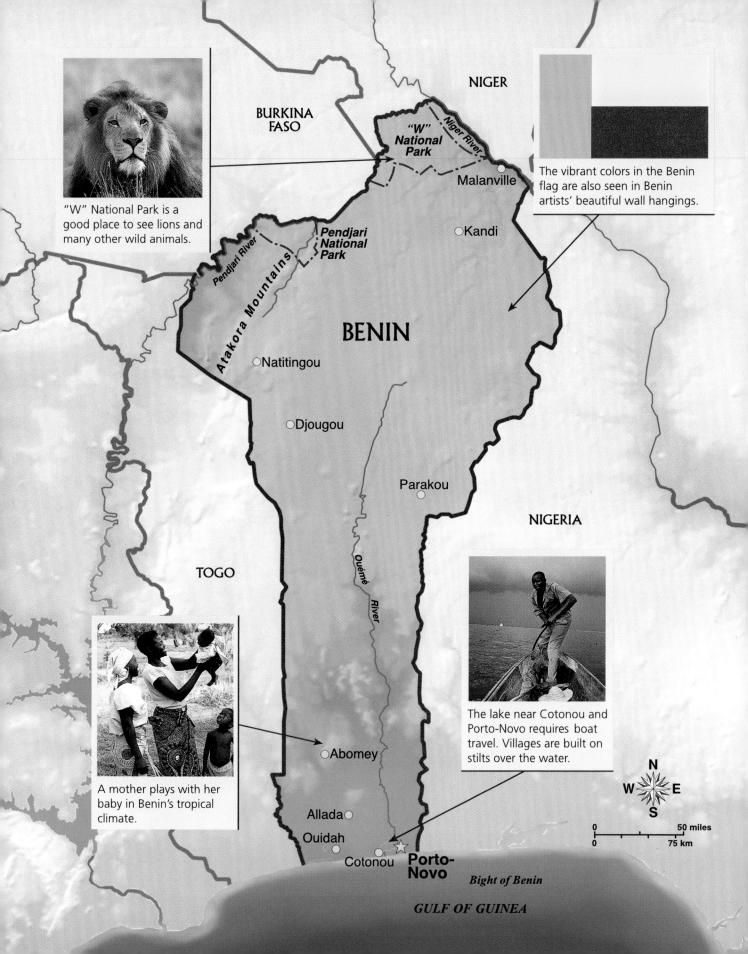

"W" National Park is a good place to see lions and many other wild animals.

The vibrant colors in the Benin flag are also seen in Benin artists' beautiful wall hangings.

NIGER

BURKINA FASO

"W" National Park

Niger River

Malanville

Kandi

Pendjari National Park

Pendjari River

Atakora Mountains

BENIN

Natitingou

Djougou

Parakou

NIGERIA

TOGO

Ouémé River

A mother plays with her baby in Benin's tropical climate.

Abomey

The lake near Cotonou and Porto-Novo requires boat travel. Villages are built on stilts over the water.

Allada

Ouidah

Cotonou

Porto-Novo

Bight of Benin

GULF OF GUINEA

N
W E
S

0   50 miles
0   75 km

Benin

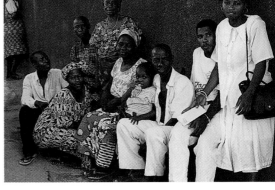

▲ This Fon family is representative of one of many ethnic groups that live in Benin.

Benin Facts

Name: Benin (Republic of Benin)
Capital: Porto-Novo
Borders: Togo, Burkina Faso, Niger, Nigeria, Bight of Benin
Population: 5,900,000
Language: Official language: French; Fon most widely spoken; others include Mina, Yoruba, Dendi
Size: 43,450 sq. mi. (112,600 sq km)
High/Low Points: Atakora Mountains, 2,103 ft. (642 km); sea level
Climate: Mild to warm along the coast with temperatures that can reach 82° F (28° C); the south has two rainy seasons separated by two dry seasons; the north has a rainy season that lasts four months, dry the remainder of the year
Wildlife: elephants, panthers, lions, monkeys, wild pigs, crocodiles, African buffalo, several species of antelope
Plants: Most of southern Benin's original rain forests have been cleared; the land is now used to grow oil palms, coconut palms, mahogony, and ebony trees.

A Country of Many Names and Faces

Benin is a small country on the West Coast of Africa. Once a territory of France, it gained independence in 1960. For many years the country was called Dahomey. The old name came from a group of people called Dahomeans, or Fons. In 1975 the name was changed to Benin after Benin City, an ancient city that flourished from the mid-1400s to the mid-1600s.

Many different ethnic groups live in Benin. They add to the country's diversity and charm. The Fon people, known for their beautiful stitched wall hangings, make up about 40 percent of the population. The Yoruba, also known for their art, live in southern and eastern Benin and in Nigeria.

The Palace that Grew and Grew... and Grew

The city of Abomey was once the capital of the great Dahomey kingdom. The first palace was built in Abomey in 1645 by a Fon king. Each king after him added onto the grounds by building his own palace. By the 1800s the palace was gigantic, and over 10,000 people lived within the grounds!

A fire destroyed all but the palaces built by the last two kings. What remains of the Abomey palace has been turned into a museum. It is considered an historic site. The outside walls are covered with sculptures that tell the history of Benin. Inside the museum you can see objects that belonged to the kings. The Room of Arms contains the carved wooden thrones of 11 kings. Some thrones are decorated with copper and silver. Behind the thrones are beautiful wall hangings.

Guardians of the King

The Abomey palace was once the largest in West Africa. The palace was unique, because at Abomey only women were used to protect the king. These women were highly respected for their skill and bravery.

◄ This photograph of Agoliagbo, King of Dahomey, now called Benin, was taken in 1870.

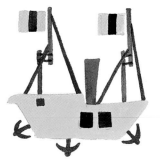

▲ Picture of a boat from a wall hanging.

The Art of Appliqué

Traditional Benin wall hangings are made using a sewing method called **appliqué.** In appliqué, small pieces of fabric are sewn on top of each other to make a picture or design. Wall hangings have bright red, yellow, green, and purple shapes of fabric sewn onto a black background. Details are added with **embroidery,** a decorative needlework used to add feathers to a bird or put a face on a monkey.

A Royal Art

Appliqué was a royal art. The beautiful wall hangings were hung on palace walls and carried in processions during ceremonies. Until the 19th century, Fon kings did not permit artists to work outside of the palace walls. These artists became the historians of the period. They created art that recorded important events of the past. Much of the art also served a spiritual purpose. Artists also created art about the king in power. Some kings asked the artists to create works that would improve their image.

Every Benin king had his own symbol carefully stitched onto wall hangings. The symbol went with a saying or story. King Tegbessu's symbol, for example, shows a buffalo wearing clothes. It goes with the saying "It is impossible to take his clothes away from him." Children learn the story behind this saying. As the story goes, Tegbessu's brothers tried to poison him to stop him from becoming king, but he was not tricked. They were not able to take his clothes, meaning his life, away from him.

Benin Fashion— A Mix of Cultures

Many people in Benin wear clothes that are like the clothing worn by people in the United States. The *agbada* is a popular outfit for men. It consists of pants, a short jacket, and a full robe. Women often wear brightly colored dresses, and many tie their hair with bandannas, or scarves. The Fon people mark their bodies with scars and work color into them in order to make their bodies beautiful.

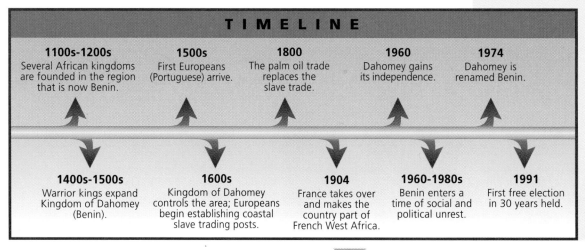

TIMELINE				
1100s-1200s Several African kingdoms are founded in the region that is now Benin.	**1500s** First Europeans (Portuguese) arrive.	**1800** The palm oil trade replaces the slave trade.	**1960** Dahomey gains its independence.	**1974** Dahomey is renamed Benin.
1400s-1500s Warrior kings expand Kingdom of Dahomey (Benin).	**1600s** Kingdom of Dahomey controls the area; Europeans begin establishing coastal slave trading posts.	**1904** France takes over and makes the country part of French West Africa.	**1960-1980s** Benin enters a time of social and political unrest.	**1991** First free election in 30 years held.

The Coastal Hub

Benin's coastline has long been a focus of activity. Benin's two main cities, Cotonou and Porto-Novo, are located on the coast. It was here that the people of Benin first made contact with people from other continents. Pictures of this geographic region can be seen in the royal symbols found in appliqués. For example, the symbol for King Agaja is a large ship. It represents the contact made with the Portuguese during his reign.

The Spread of Culture

The West Coast of Africa also made the region an easy stopping place for slave-traders. Over 350 years ago, the Dahomey kingdom became rich by selling slaves to traders. For over 100 years, about 10,000 slaves a year were shipped to Brazil, the Caribbean, and Haiti. Southern Benin became known as the Slave Coast. This uprooting of black people caused a spread of African culture to many parts of the world. Today, parts of African religion, music, and art can be found in the places where slavery once existed.

Myths and Truths of Voodoo

The religion of voodoo has its roots in West Africa. The word *voodoo* came from the Fon people and means "spirit." It spread from Benin and surrounding countries to Haiti, the Dominican Republic, and parts of the United States. Voodoo provides a way of life for many people in Benin. Voodoo followers worship many spirits and **deities,** or gods. About 70 percent of Benin's population practice **animism,** the belief that all things in nature have a spirit. The Yoruba people, for example, believe that spirits are found everywhere—in rocks, rivers, trees, and songs.

▲ Both traditional Benin culture and the influence of Western culture can be seen in this photo of a man cooking in a marketplace.

Festival in Progress

Benin is known for its lively dances and festivals. Traditional dances may give thanks, express joy or sorrow, or be religious in nature. A lucky traveler in Benin might even see a crowd of people running joyfully down a road after what seems to be a dancing haystack! It is simply a dance in progress. Tourists are welcome to follow along!

Yoruba Art

The Yoruba made bronze heads of their kings using a process called *lost wax casting*. The process uses clay and beeswax to make a mold that is eventually put into a fire. The beeswax melts away and is replaced by very hot, liquid metal. When the metal hardens, the sculpture is completed. To make these works of art, the Yoruba would melt down their most valuable money, C-shaped metal bars called *manillas*. The finished sculptures were used as decorations to fill the king's palace.

Home Sweet Home

In modern cities like Cotonou, many people live in concrete houses. In the countryside, where most of the population lives, people live in simple houses built by hand. Houses are usually grouped in villages. Each house consists of several rooms and a courtyard. The walls, called *wattles*, are made of woven sticks that are plastered with mud.

Stools are one of the most important and unusual pieces of furniture in many Benin houses. Men use beautifully decorated, carved stools that are made from a single piece of wood. The stools women use are just a few inches tall. They carry their stools with them wherever they go, so they always have a place to sit. Wood-carving is a respected art form in Benin. Skilled craftspeople are known for their carved wood masks, tables, armchairs, and stools.

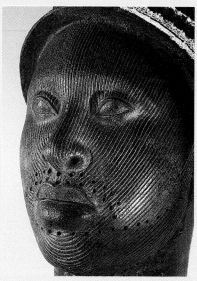

▲ Yoruba artists sculpted bronze heads of their kings using a process called lost wax casting.

◀ Benin artisans are known for their beautiful carved wood stools.

Twins

The Yoruba people of Benin and Nigeria have the highest rate of twin births in the world. The twin who is born first is considered to be younger. It is believed that he or she was sent first to inspect the world for the older twin. Many patterns in Yoruba art are given special importance by being *twinned,* or doubled.

Wildlife with a "W"

Today, one of Benin's treasures is the "W" National Park. This enormous park spreads into three countries (Benin, Niger, Burkina Faso), but nearly half of its 2,800,000 acres (1,132,000 ha) are found in Benin. The park was named because of its location near a "w"-shaped bend in the nearby Niger River. The river is filled with hippos, African buffaloes, and elephants.

Baboons, patas monkeys, jackals, hyenas, and lions live in the park's forests. Cheetahs, leopards, and wildcats, like the serval, can also be spotted in the park, but they are not as common. Pendjari, Benin's other national park, is also popular with tourists. It is less than half the size of "W."

Animal Watching

The best time to visit Benin's national parks is in the very early morning when animals gather at the water holes. Even then, spotting wildlife can be hard. On a bad day there may only be a few wart hogs! Even so, looking for animals is half the fun of going to these parks.

Wild animals represent many of ancient Dahomey's kings in wall hangings. A buffalo symbolizes King Gezo, one of Dahomey's former leaders. The selection of this animal to represent the king shows his strength and power.

▲ African buffaloes share their home along the Niger River in "W" National Park with a large population of hippos and elephants.

African Elephants

"W" Park has about 850 African elephants. They are larger and more fierce than Asiatic elephants. The largest known African elephant weighed about 12 tons. They have very large ears that can be up to 4 feet (1.2 m) wide, with smooth foreheads and large, curved trunks. The tusks of the bulls can weigh 50 to 100 pounds (23-45 kg) each.

▲ The pictures in Benin's colorful wall hangings tell a story.

A Textile Tradition

Benin's appliqué wall hangings speak a language of pictures. Although appliqués are no longer made as royal art, they are still popular in Benin and are easy to find.

History Lessons

Every Fon parent in Benin is responsible for teaching the children the meanings of the images in the wall hangings. As Fon children learn the meaning of the pictures, they also learn the history of their country.

People who make the wall hangings use old, familiar symbols, as well as adding new pictures that are important to their lives today. The symbols used in these story cloths may be common, everyday objects that have been given special meaning. The cloth workers keep the patterns so they can reuse patterns that are important to them or to their family. In this way, Benin wall hangings are a living history of old and new pictures and stories that continue to be told and retold.

Benin is a young country. Almost one-half of the population is under the age of 15! **Literacy** is a problem in Benin. About 63 percent of Benin's population cannot read or write. One way of passing down and sharing important information is through storytelling and art.

A Pineapple Legend

In Benin the pineapple is known as a symbol of good luck. This is because of one king's story. King Agonglo was standing under a palm tree one day when suddenly it began to storm. The tree was struck by lightning, but Agonglo was not hurt. He compared himself to the pineapple, telling his people that lightning may strike the palm tree but is powerless against its fruit. According to this legend, pineapples are never struck by lightning.

Pineapple image from a wall hanging

Tools

- pencil
- colored pencils
- fabric scissors
- tape measure
- iron
- pins
- chalk or non-permanent fabric marking pen
- needles (embroidery or quilting)

Materials

- typing paper
- one large piece of butcher paper
- tape
- 1 yd. (1 m) of a solid color background fabric
- small pieces of lightweight cotton fabrics in solid colors
- sewing threads
- embroidery floss or thin cotton yarns
- dowel or rod
- string or ribbon

Plan the Story Cloth Pictures

4-5. Plan the banner shape.

Make a wall hanging covered with colorful symbol pictures that tell a story about you.

Plan the Story Cloth Pictures

To make a story cloth banner, you will use the sewing method called appliqué. In appliqué, you cut scraps of cloth into shapes. Then you stitch them onto a background fabric. Plan the picture carefully before you begin to sew.

1. First, choose a theme for your banner. You might want to focus on your hobbies, interests, or parts of your personality. You could make a banner of people and animals that are important to you. Or, you might picture an important event in your life.

2. Draw three to five different images that help to illustrate your theme. Use shapes of people, animals, or objects. Use only images that are important to the story you want to tell. Each image will be separate from other pictures on the background cloth.

3. Now, redraw each image on white typing paper. Draw simple, rounded shapes that will be easy to cut out and sew. Read the hints for ideas about the size and shape of the images.

4. The shape of the banner is up to you. It can be vertical or horizontal, wide or narrow. Cut around the drawings, and spread them out on a large piece of paper. Space the images evenly apart from each other. *(See diagram.)*

5. When you are satisfied with the placement, tape the drawings down on the background paper. Cut around the outside to make the final size and shape of the banner. Refer to this plan as you sew your banner. *(See diagram.)*

Story Cloth Hints

- Make the images big and bold so that they can be seen from a distance. Draw small parts, such as eyes, larger than normal.

- Make all shapes, including arms and legs, compact, not stretched out. They will be easier to sew and will look stronger.

- Add small details and lines with simple embroidery stitches.

Color Hints

- Use colors that contrast, or stand out from each other, so that each part of the banner will be easy to see.

- Use each color in several different places on the banner, so it will have a unified, or whole, look.

- Make creative color choices! Animals and objects do not need to be their real-life colors.

Plan the Colors

Carefully plan the colors for your story cloth. Stick to a simple color plan. Read the Color Hints on this page.

1. Choose the fabric you will use for the background. In Benin, story cloth banners often have black, gold, or white backgrounds. Pick a background fabric that will help the colors of your story pictures to stand out.

2. Choose about six solid-color fabrics for the story pictures. (Sometimes you might want to use a small amount of print fabric to add interest.) Cut small scraps of each fabric. Lay them out on the background fabric to see how they look together.

3. Look at your banner drawing again. Use colored pencils to color the story pictures the colors of the fabrics you have chosen. Draw dotted lines to show any details to be added with embroidery stitches. *(See diagram.)*

Sew Your Banner

1. Measure the size of the banner from your drawing. Add an extra four inches (10 cm) at the top to wrap around a rod or dowel. Measure and cut the background cloth. Fold the top edge under and sew a hem to hold the rod or dowel. *(See diagram.)*

2. Make the pattern pieces for one of your story cloth pictures. Trace or redraw each part of the image onto another piece of paper. Cut out all of the pattern pieces and label them. *(See diagram.)*

3. Next, iron the first piece of fabric. Lay the pattern piece on the fabric, leaving room for an extra 1/2-inch (1.2-cm) on all sides. Pin the pattern down in a few places. *(See diagram.)*

◄ Sew the story cloth pieces onto the background cloth.

Plan the Colors

3. Color the pictures.

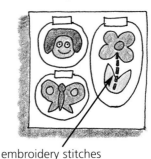

embroidery stitches

Sew Your Banner

1. Cut the background fabric.

4 in. (10 cm)

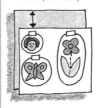

2. Make the pattern pieces.

3. Pin the pattern down.

Stitches You Will Use

Thread a needle and tie a knot at the end of the thread. You may use a single or double thread. Start sewing from the back of the background fabric so that the knot will be hidden.

backstitch – Take a small stitch backwards. Sew up again in front of your first stitch. Stitch back to fill in the space. Repeat.

running stitch – Sew in and out of the fabric in a straight line. Make stitches that are even in length.

tack stitch – Take a tiny stitch over the edge of the picture piece into the background fabric. Pull the thread tight. Repeat.

backstitch

running stitch

tack stitch

4. Trace around the pattern with chalk or a non-permanent fabric marking pen. Remove the pins and cut out the shape, 1/2-inch (1.2-cm) outside the marked line. Repeat for all the parts of the first story picture. *(See diagram.)*

5. Pin the bottom piece of the first picture to the background fabric. Check your plan to find the right place. Clip curved edges and points as illustrated. This will allow them to turn under smoothly. Fold the edges under and press them flat with your finger. *(See diagram.)*

6. Sew the piece to the background. Use a *tack stitch* or a *running stitch,* shown above. Remove the pins. Add the next shape and sew it down. Continue to cut and sew until all the pictures have been sewn to the background cloth. *(See diagram.)* (See photograph on page 24.)

7. Add lines and details with embroidery stitches. Use embroidery floss or thin cotton yarn in colors that contrast with the fabric colors. Use simple embroidery stitches, such as the *running stitch* or the *backstitch.*

8. Iron your story cloth banner. Slip a dowel or rod in the hem and tie a string or ribbon to the ends. Hang your banner on the wall. *(See diagram.)*

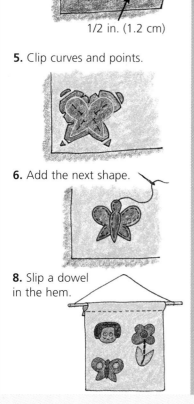

4. Trace and cut out the shape.

cutting line

1/2 in. (1.2 cm)

5. Clip curves and points.

6. Add the next shape.

8. Slip a dowel in the hem.

Other Ideas

■ Sew a banner using felt for the story pictures. You don't need to turn the edges under, because felt will not fray.

These finished ▶ banners tell stories with symbol pictures.

NAMIBIA

Johannesburg has been called the City of Gold, because more than a mile under its crowded streets miners are hard at work.

A wide variety of animals, including the hippopotamus, are protected in Kruger National Park.

ZIMBABWE

BOTSWANA

MOZAMBIQUE

Kalahari Desert

Kruger National Park

SOUTH AFRICA

Johannesburg ☆ **Pretoria** (Executive)
Soweto

SWAZILAND

Vaal River

K w a Z u l u Natal

○ Welkom

Champagne Castle

Orange River

○ Kimberley

☆
Bloemfontein (Judicial)

Caledon River

LESOTHO

▲ Tugela River

Orange River

Drakensberg Mountains

ATLANTIC OCEAN

New Bethesda ○

Great Karroo

Cape Ranges

East London ○

Cape Town ☆ (Legislative)

Cape of Good Hope

Port Elizabeth ○

Cape Town's waterfront is a lively area with shops, craft markets, hotels, and restaurants.

INDIAN OCEAN

In 1996, South Africa's new constitution became law. It ensured equal rights for all South Africans.

N W E S

0 ——— 200 miles
0 ——— 300 km

South Africa Facts

Name: Republic of South Africa
Capital: Cape Town (legislative),
Pretoria (executive),
Bloemfontein (judicial)
Borders: Lesotho, Botswana,
Mozambique, Namibia, Swaziland,
Zimbabwe, Indian Ocean,
Atlantic Ocean
Population: About 40 million
Language: 11 official languages:
Afrikaans, English, Ndebele, North
Sesotho, South Sesotho, Swazi,
Tsonga, Tswana, Venda, Xhosa,
and Zulu
Major Ethnic/National Groups:
76 percent black (mainly Zulu,
Xhosa, Sotho, and Tswana);
13 percent white; 9 percent
colored people of mixed descent;
2 percent Asian
Size: 471,445 sq. mi.
(1,221,037 sq km)
High/Low Point: Champagne
Castle, 11,072 ft. (3,375 m); sea
level along the coast
Climate: Most of South Africa
has a mild, sunny climate; summer
temperatures may reach 104° F
(40° C); winter temperatures in
some parts may drop below
freezing; only about one-fourth of
the country gets over 25 inches
(64 cm) of rain a year, mostly in
the summer except in the Cape
Mountains region
Wildlife: Elephants, giraffes, lions,
ostriches, zebras, wildebeest, mostly
found on reserves; 900 species
of birds
Plants: More than 22,000 species.
South Africa is the only country
with one of the world's six plant
kingdoms, named the Cape
kingdom, in the Western Cape,
with over 8,500 native plants,
most found only in South Africa.

South Africa

▲ Table Mountain forms a backdrop for the city of Cape Town.

A World in One Country

From the interior plateau, a raised, level land surface, to the mountains and the coastal areas, South Africa is a land of great contrasts. Geologists believe that over 200 million years ago the stretch and pull of the earth's surface created a necklace of high peaks that rise gracefully, protecting the fertile valleys below.

Table Mountain in the center of Cape Town is South Africa's best-known landmark. A cable car takes visitors to the top, which looks like a big flat table. In winter a thick white fog often hides the mountain from view. This fog, commonly called "the tablecloth," actually looks more like a puffy white comforter.

South Africa has many national parks and animal reserves. Kruger National Park is located in the northeast part of the plateau. It has elephants, lions, zebras, and leopards. This park is South Africa's most popular tourist attraction.

Diamonds in the Dust

In contrast, the *karoo*, the desert area that covers one-third of South Africa, seems even more dry and desolate. Yet, it was here in Kimberley in 1867 that 15-year-old Erasmus Jacobs found diamonds. Kimberley's Big Hole became the largest human-made crater, or hole, dug by hand. It yielded three tons of diamonds before it closed in 1914. At that time it had reached a depth of 3,600 feet (1,097 m).

Not long after the discovery of diamonds, gold was found beneath the city of Johannesburg. South Africa is still the world's leading supplier of gold and other minerals. Unfortunately, these minerals led many white people in South Africa to become wealthy and black people to become poorer.

This replica of the original diamond- ▶ mining settlement at Kimberley forms part of the Kimberley Mine Museum.

Who is South African?

The variety in South Africa's landscape is mirrored in the many different people who are, in fact, South African. Some anthropologists, scientists who study the origin and development of human beings, believe that the San people have lived in Southern Africa for more than 40,000 years. Much later, Bantu-speaking people began to arrive in KwaZulu-Natal. It was not until the 1400s that Portuguese explorer Bartolomeu Dias sailed around the Cape of Good Hope. Two hundred years later, the Dutch arrived in Table Bay, Cape Town. They found the southern coast a handy stopping point on their way to India. The British began to occupy the Cape in 1795, creating white settlements all over South Africa. In 1908-1909, an all-white convention created a "unified country." However, they did not consult the vast majority of black people in South Africa, who had practically no rights under the new state.

▲ This Zulu basket weaver represents one of the many different tribal groups that call South Africa their home.

Apartheid Means "Separateness"

South Africa will forever be remembered for its system of **apartheid** (uh PAHR tāt). This was the white South African government's policy of racial **segregation** and political and economic **discrimination** that began in 1910. Apartheid means "separateness" in the Afrikaans language, and it lived up to its name. During the next 80 years, apartheid laws and policies kept white and black people separate from each other. It also kept some nonwhite groups apart from other groups. Whites were given the best land, the best schools, and the best jobs. Eventually, the world reacted with outrage to apartheid. The United Nations banned the sale of arms, or weapons, to South Africa. The U.S. Congress imposed stiff economic **sanctions,** or penalties, and foreign banks refused to give South Africa any new loans. South Africans were not allowed to take part in international sports or cultural events, including the Olympics or the World Cup, until apartheid ended.

Nelson Mandela, Former President of South Africa

From political prisoner to president of South Africa, Nelson Mandela is a highly respected and beloved leader. He was arrested for his political views in 1962. In 1990, after 27 years in prison, he was finally released. He was awarded the Nobel Peace Prize in 1993. A year later, after the country's first free election, Nelson Mandela became the first president of the new South Africa.

Township Life

Apartheid created *townships* as places where only black people could live. Today, although apartheid has officially ended, most blacks still live in townships. Some stay by choice, but others stay because they do not have the money to move. South Western Township, or Soweto, is a very large city. Townships also exist near Cape Town and in other parts of South Africa.

▲ Most of South Africa's black citizens still live in crowded townships.

Under apartheid, townships had few basic services. There was no mail delivery. Each house had one garbage pail, no matter how many people lived in the house. The government is now slowly working to bring services to everyone. Schools are improving. Much of Soweto, for example, now has electricity, clinics, and even a sports stadium.

Art and Politics

South African art and politics are tied together. During apartheid, poets often read their poetry at political rallies. Today there is still a close connection between building a new nation and the art it produces. "Black theater" combines words, music, singing, and dance. It is created by and for mostly black audiences. It tells of life under apartheid as well as other more general themes.

South African art and music are a wonderful mix of urban, rural, and native, or original, ways of life. "Choral bands" like Ladysmith Black Mambazo have become popular worldwide. Artist Tito Nungu creates skyscrapers and airplanes in a style like African beadwork.

▲ Life is difficult for people living in townships, like this one near Cape Town.

Where in the World Are We?

South African maps drawn before 1994 left townships off the map. Directions to a house or highway had to be given by word of mouth.

TIMELINE

about 40,000 B.C.
San people settle in Southern Africa.

1488
Portuguese navigator Bartolomeu Dias sails around the Cape of Good Hope.

1806
England takes control of the Cape from Holland.

1867
Diamonds are discovered near Kimberley.

1976
20,000 students stage a nonviolent demonstration in support of Afrikaans as the language of instruction. Police use tear gas and bullets, killing several people, which produced mass riots.

1996
On December 10, the new constitution becomes law, ensuring equal rights for all South Africans.

300 A.D.
Bantu people arrive in the KwaZulu-Natal area.

1652
Dutch settlers arrive at Table Bay, Cape Town.

1834
Slavery is abolished.

1910
Union of South Africa is formed.

1963
Nelson Mandela is sentenced to life in prison.

1994
Nelson Mandela becomes the country's first democratically elected president.

1999
Thabo Mbeki becomes South Africa's second freely elected president, succeeding Mandela.

Little to Spare

In the townships, where there is little to spare, recycling is a way of life. Empty beverage cans are hammered down and joined together. They gain new life as a lunch boxes, guitars, candlesticks, and picture frames. Shoelaces become belts, and wire is bent into bowls and toys. Everything is used again and again.

The making of beautiful items out of everyday materials is actually an ancient art form that is found in many different cultures and geographic areas. In South Africa, however, the creating of wire toys, candleholders, and soap dishes is relatively new.

Children as Artisans

Children in the townships are credited with making the first wire toys. Wire coat hangers and wire thread are readily available. Older boys teach younger children how to make small tricycles and cars out of wire. They make sure that the wheels roll and the doors open. Some toys are made just for fun. Other toys are made to sell.

It is not unusual to see young men selling wire toys on street corners and on traffic islands where people make purchases out of their car windows. People often buy these wire toys to take as gifts to friends they are about to visit. Township art, once looked down upon, is now very popular. With the increase in tourists, many people are becoming interested in these beautiful and interesting wire sculptures.

South Africa Honors Its Youth

In South Africa, June 16th is National Youth Day. Young people led the way in South Africa's freedom struggle. People of all ages are convinced that nothing would have changed in South Africa without the courage and positive thinking of its young people. In addition to being a legal holiday, National Youth Day, once known as Soweto Day, is slated to become election day.

◄ Children in South Africa are credited with making the first wire toys. This toy was made by someone in Soweto.

Tools

- pencil
- snub-nosed and needle-nosed pliers
- wire cutters
- permanent marking pen
- scissors
- clothespins

Materials

- wire (spools of 14-, 16-, 18-, and 20-gauge wire, available at hardware stores)
- paper
- duct tape
- strips of stretch fabrics or florist's tape
- white craft glue
- cardboard scraps

Plan Your Wire Toy

3. Plan the axle.

one pedal

two pedals

4. Draw a pattern for the axle.

4-5 in. (10-12.5 cm)

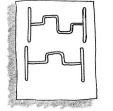

two pedals

one pedal

Use your creativity to build a wire toy with moving parts.

Collect the Wire

In addition to the recommended spools of wire, collect other pieces of wire. Look for thin copper wire, plastic-coated electrical wire, colored florist's wire, soft aluminum wire, brass wire, and even pipe cleaners. Coat hangers (about 12-gauge) are hard to bend, but they are very strong. Bend and twist each kind of wire to see what it can do.

Plan Your Wire Toy

1. Decide what kind of toy you will make. It could be a person who beats a drum or pedals a cart. It could be an animal that jumps, or a bird that flaps its wings.

2. Plan the body of your toy. Draw a picture of its wire shape. What will you use to cover the body? Study the Wire Toy Hints for ideas.

3. Plan the axle, the shaft between the wheels that will make the parts move. The simplest axle has one pedal. It raises and lowers parts of the toy as the wheel turns. An axle with two pedals will raise and lower two parts, one after the other. *(See diagram.)*

4. Draw a pattern for your axle. Leave a four- to five-inch (10 – 12.5 cm) space between the wheels. Draw the pedal or pedals in the center of the axle. Leave room on each side of the axle to attach the base. *(See diagram.)*

Wire Toy Hints

- The body is a simple wire framework. It can be covered with cloth, felt, or colored florist's tape.

- The moving parts can be made of wires that are looped around the body. They can also be made of cardboard that is taped to the body.

looped wire arms

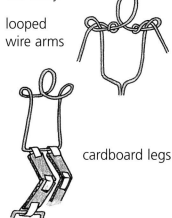

cardboard legs

- The moving parts need to be located right above the pedals that move them. They need to have room to move freely.

Make the Wheels

1. Now you're ready to make the wheels! They should be large enough to keep the pedals from hitting the ground. Find a solid round object, a bottle or can, to use as a form.

2. The wheels and axle are made from a long, stiff piece of wire—14-gauge wire works well. Wrap one end of the wire around the form to make the first wheel rim. Overlap the end as shown. Slide the wire off the form. *(See diagram.)*

3. Bend the wire straight into the center of the wheel to make a spoke. To make a sharp turn, grasp the wire with pliers. Push the wire down squarely over the edge of the pliers with your hand. *(See diagram.)*

4. Use your pattern as a guide to form the axle and the pedals. Measure each bend, and make a mark on the wire with a permanent marking pen. *(See diagram.)*

5. Measure and mark the second spoke to be the same length as the first spoke. Before you bend this spoke, form the second wheel. Then bend the second spoke. *(See diagram.)*

6. Overlap the end of the wire a little, and then cut off any extra wire. Use a small piece of duct tape to join the ends of the wires to the wheel rims where they overlap. Adjust the wheels and axle until they are round. *(See diagram.)*

7. Wrap the wheels to give them traction, or friction. Cut a long strip of thin stretch fabric. Cover one wire spoke with white craft glue. Wrap the fabric around the spoke down to the center of the wheel. Stretch the cloth across to the rim to create another spoke, as shown. *(See diagram.)*

8. Continue to wrap the strip tightly around the rim of the wheel. Clip the end of the strip with a clothespin until the glue dries. (Note: You can use florist's tape instead of fabric and glue.)

◀ Students form wheels and wrap them.

Make the Wheels

2. Form the wheel rim.

3. Bend the spoke.

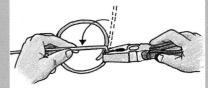

4. Bend the axle and pedals.

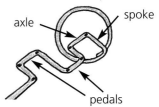

axle   spoke   pedals

5. Form the second wheel.

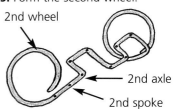

2nd wheel   2nd axle   2nd spoke

6. Join the wires to the wheel rims.

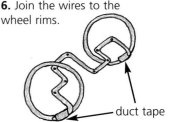

duct tape

7. Wrap the wheels.

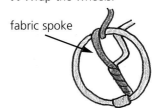

fabric spoke

Build the Body

1. Make the base.

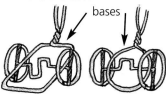

bases

2. Form the body.

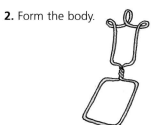

3. Attach the base to the axle.

axle

4-5. Make the moving parts, and attach them to the pedals.

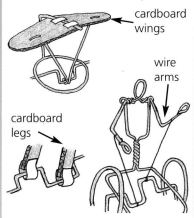

cardboard wings

wire arms

cardboard legs

6. Make a long handle.

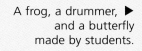

Build the Body

Put on your creative thinking hat to make the body of your wire toy. To make it strong, form the body and base from one long piece of strong wire. Decide where you will start and end the wire. If you need to twist wires together, put the connections in places that will not have stress on them.

1. Begin by forming a rectangular or a round base. Make it narrow enough to fit easily between the wheels. Test to be sure that the pedals can turn within the space. *(See diagram.)*

2. Next, form the body. Hold it on the wheels every so often as you work. Check to make sure that you have room for the moving parts above the pedals. *(See diagram.)*

3. Wrap the base with strips of cloth or florist's tape. Attach the base to the axle with two short pieces of 20-gauge wire as shown. The base should balance on the axle, and the wheels should turn freely. *(See diagram.)*

4. Make the moving parts from cardboard or wire. This will be a process of trial and error. Hold them in place to see if they will work. When you are satisfied, tape cardboard wings or legs to the body. Slide wire arms through the shoulder loop, and twist loosely. *(See diagram.)*

5. Attach the moving parts to the pedals. Loop feet around the pedals, or extend a wire up to the arms or wings. Test the toy and adjust it until it moves easily when you push it. Wire toys usually work better on a carpet than on a smooth floor. *(See diagram.)*

6. To finish your toy, cover the wire body with fabric, felt, or florist's tape. Attach recycled objects, such as bottle caps, string, and scraps of rubber. Make a long handle of strong wire twisted firmly to the base. *(See diagram.)*

A frog, a drummer, ▶ and a butterfly made by students.

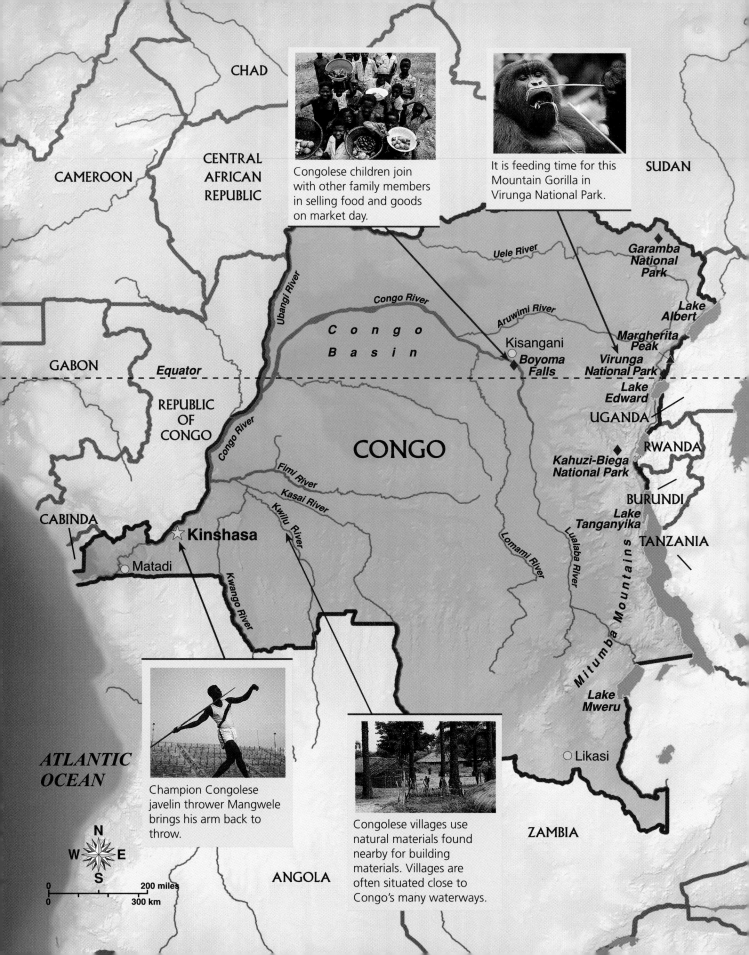

CHAD

CAMEROON

CENTRAL AFRICAN REPUBLIC

SUDAN

Congolese children join with other family members in selling food and goods on market day.

It is feeding time for this Mountain Gorilla in Virunga National Park.

Uele River

Congo River

C o n g o   B a s i n

Ubangi River

Aruwimi River

Garamba National Park

Lake Albert

Kisangani
Boyoma Falls

Margherita Peak

Virunga National Park

GABON

Equator

REPUBLIC OF CONGO

Congo River

CONGO

Lake Edward

UGANDA

RWANDA

Kahuzi-Biega National Park

Fimi River

Kasai River

Kwilu River

Lomami River

Lualaba River

BURUNDI

Lake Tanganyika

TANZANIA

CABINDA

★ Kinshasa

Matadi

Kwango River

M i t u m b a   M o u n t a i n s

Lake Mweru

ATLANTIC OCEAN

Champion Congolese javelin thrower Mangwele brings his arm back to throw.

Congolese villages use natural materials found nearby for building materials. Villages are often situated close to Congo's many waterways.

○ Likasi

ZAMBIA

N
W   E
S

0 ___ 200 miles
0 ___ 300 km

ANGOLA

Congo

The Land of Adventure

The exact location of the cartoon and movie character Tarzan's tropical home in Africa has always been a mystery. Because of its beauty and the wildness of the land, the Congo, formerly Zaire, has been called the African country most likely to be Tarzan's home.

▲ The Congo River is a lifeline to the Congolese people. The river provides a means of travel and trade. It also supplies water needed to grow their crops.

Congo is also called the Democratic Republic of the Congo. The equator passes through the northern part of the country in the heart of the African tropical rain forest. This beautiful country is perhaps better suited for adventurers than for sightseers. Deep rain forests, **savannas,** volcanic mountains, and the great Congo River make traveling in the Congo an explorer's dream. But this kind of travel is difficult for most visitors. It can take a month to get from one end of the country to the other. Available transportation takes visitors on poor roads, slow riverboats, infrequent trains, or on rides in the back of trucks. Political violence has also made the country a dangerous place for travelers. Yet everyone who returns from the Congo has a exciting story to tell and a sense of wonder at its beauty.

Kinshasa

Walking through the marketplace in the Congo's modern capital city, Kinshasa, is an adventure in itself. There are many interesting sights, sounds, and smells. Buyers and sellers wear many different styles of colorful tribal clothing. Vendors call out *"mbuya, mbuya,"* which means "mask" in the Lingala language. They are eager to sell visitors their beautiful wooden masks. The sound of music also fills the marketplace. Kinshasa is known as a center of African pop music. Smells of cooking spices, peanuts, meat, and rice come from the food vendors preparing *moambé*, the national dish.

◄ Market day in Kinshasa is a busy time. Vendors sell food, musicians play popular music, and cooks prepare traditional foods.

Congo Facts

Name: Congo or Democratic Republic of the Congo (formerly Zaire)
Capital: Kinshasa
Borders: Republic of Congo, Central African Republic, Sudan, Uganda, Rwanda, Burundi, Tanzania, Zambia, Angola
Population: Over 47 million; more than 200 tribes
Language: Official language: French. Many tribal languages, including Lingala, Swahili, Tshiluba, Konga
Size: 905,354 sq. mi. (2,345,409 sq km), Third largest country in Africa
Highest/Lowest Point: Margherita Peak 16,762 ft. (5,109 m); sea level
Climate: Hot and humid in the tropical north and west (about 90° F/32° C); cooler and drier in the south and east (70-75° F/21-24° C)
Wildlife: 1,000 species of birds; a wide variety of rare and endangered animals, including mountain and eastern lowland gorillas, white rhinos, okapi, an animal related to the giraffe, and the African manatee
Plants: In the Congo rain forest, 1,500 species of flowering plants and 750 species of trees

The Congo River

Since ancient times, the lives of the people of the Congo have been tied to water. Water enabled people to grow crops and to journey from one place to another. Traveling on the Congo River from Kinshasa to Kisangani by riverboat is an unforgettable experience. The boat, a steamer with many barges tied together, is like a floating village. As many as 2,000 people may be on board. Music plays and people dance throughout the night. People in market stalls sell a variety of items, including food, monkeys, and other animals.

Riverboat travelers today follow ancient routes established by the area's earliest people, who settled in the Congo River basin about 2,000 years ago. Among others, the Bantu-speaking peoples made the Congo their home. They were hunters and gatherers who began to grow crops in the rich soil. About 1,000 B.C., they began to develop their own culture and system of beliefs. They formed kingdoms with strong rulers and spiritual practices that used masks. Throughout the Congo's long history, its people have passed down many ancient tribal beliefs and ceremonies.

A Land of Many Resources

The Congo's culture and nature-based beliefs were influenced by the region's natural resources. Water and oil are potentially rich sources of energy. The Congolese rain forest is another natural resource. The rain forest contains many varieties of plants, animals, insects, and birds. The Congolese people use rain forest wood for firewood and to carve their religious masks, just as they did in ancient times.

Congo Basin

The huge Congo Basin rain forest covers about one-third of the country and accounts for one-half of all the woodlands in Africa. Until recently, it remained mostly un-touched. Now the edges of this massive area are being deforested, or logged, to make way for roads, buildings, and more farmland.

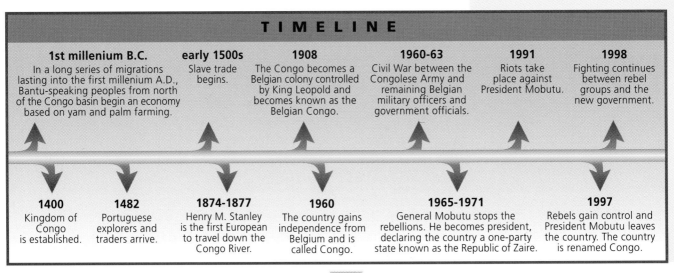

TIMELINE

1st millenium B.C.
In a long series of migrations lasting into the first millenium A.D., Bantu-speaking peoples from north of the Congo basin begin an economy based on yam and palm farming.

early 1500s
Slave trade begins.

1908
The Congo becomes a Belgian colony controlled by King Leopold and becomes known as the Belgian Congo.

1960-63
Civil War between the Congolese Army and remaining Belgian military officers and government officials.

1991
Riots take place against President Mobutu.

1998
Fighting continues between rebel groups and the new government.

1400
Kingdom of Congo is established.

1482
Portuguese explorers and traders arrive.

1874-1877
Henry M. Stanley is the first European to travel down the Congo River.

1960
The country gains independence from Belgium and is called Congo.

1965-1971
General Mobutu stops the rebellions. He becomes president, declaring the country a one-party state known as the Republic of Zaire.

1997
Rebels gain control and President Mobutu leaves the country. The country is renamed Congo.

Congo Tribal Groups

There are over 200 tribal groups in the Congo. Four-fifths of them are Bantu. Other tribal groups range from the Tutsi, once one of the tallest people on earth, to the Pygmies, who are the shortest people.

The Pygmy people have lived in the rain forests of Africa for thousands of years. Pygmies usually average about 4.5 feet (1.4 m) tall. Because they are so short, they can walk easily under many of the thick vines and trees that grow in the rain forests, while taller people must crawl on their hands and knees. Adventurers visiting the Congo can arrange to go on a hunting trip with the Pygmies and visit their villages in the Kahuzi-Biega National Park. They have been known to perform masked dances for guests.

A Wealth of Wildlife

Thousands of different species of animals, reptiles, and birds live in the Congo. They are a priceless natural resource. Many of these species are now in national parks where they are protected from extinction, or dying out. Garamba National Park protects the rare northern white rhino. In 1984, before they came under the protection of the park, only 15 of these beautiful animals remained. About 20 families of eastern lowland gorillas live in Kahuzi-Biega National Park. Mountain gorillas are protected at Virunga National Park. It is one of the oldest reserves in Africa and is thought to be the best game park. Lake Edward, part of the park, has one of the world's largest remaining groups of hippos. Unfortunately, the unstable political situation in the Congo has made the region unsafe for travel. As a result, Virunga has been closed to tourism.

The magnificent wildlife of the Congo inspires its artists. Animals are represented in Congolese masks, sculptures, and in dance ceremonies. Leopards, apes, and owls are popular mask designs.

▲ The rare northern white rhino is protected in Congo's Garamba National Park.

Spirits and Religion

About 70 percent of the people in the Congo practice Christianity. However, the Congolese also believe that everything in life is religious. They believe that God created everything with a spirit force. These spirits live everywhere—in the sky, sun, earth, water, rocks, animals, and trees. Thunder and lightning, a house, and ancestors all have spirits. The powerful spirits in all things can produce good or evil for human beings. This belief in spirits is called animism. The people of the Congo use art, including masks, in rituals, or ceremonies, to make sure that the spirits work toward their well-being and protection.

Masked Spirits

Since ancient times, Congolese masks have been made to stand for spirits. The people of the Congo believe that masked dancers bring these spirits into the real world. The spirits come to protect, educate, heal, discipline, and support people through all the changes in human life.

Masks are usually made, worn, and cared for by men. Often these honored men in the community form secret groups to guard the masks and the special ceremonies in which they are used. The Congolese people believe that if the masks are not kept secret, their special power will be lost.

The Masker

The person who wears a mask during a village event or ceremony is called a masker. When a masker puts on his mask, the Congolese people believe his own identity disappears. He takes on the identity of the spirit that the mask represents.

The mask is often part of a larger costume that covers the masker's whole body. The mask itself can cover the face or the entire head. It is carved and decorated to represent a human face or the features of an animal. Masks may combine the features of several animals or be part animal and part human.

Maskers serve many purposes at different events. Maskers are asked to safely bring in the change of seasons or to control nature and ensure good crops. Maskers dance at times of great change in people's lives. They may appear as guides to the next world when a person is dying. Maskers are called to take the form of wise ancestors when there is a problem in the village. Maskers also take part in healing ceremonies.

Congolese people believe that ▶ during tribal ceremonies, masked dancers have the power to bring spirits into the real world to protect and help them. In this photo, a Kuba man wears a special ceremonial mask for a dance. The Kuba tribe is now extinct.

This oval mask is worn by a tribal dancer ready for a festival.

Some Lega tribe ceremonies include carved masks that represent a person's level of achievement.

The Masked Dances

The people of the Congo believe that dancing increases the power of the masked performers. The quick movements, songs, and sounds work together with the masked costume to create a powerful and energetic force. Many masked dances are exciting and noisy. There may be drumming and quick leaps in the air. A masker often dances a story from the tribe's history.

Changing from Child to Adult

Masks play an important role in rituals that mark a **rite of passage,** or an important life change. One rite of passage is the change from child to adult. Masks are worn by male guides when they take boys in the village from their mothers to a place outside the village. Here the ceremony that leads the boys into adulthood begins. Masks are used by the older guides as they teach the boys how to hunt, make and use tools, and how to defend the village. Masked elders also teach the boys about their honored ancestors and the power of the spirit world.

The boys wear special masks when the ritual is over, and they are welcomed back into the community as adults. Small pendant masks, worn around the neck as a necklace or hanging from a belt, are often presented to the boys. These special pendant masks mark the successful completion of the rite of passage.

This Kuba mask has cowrie shells sewn on to fabric. Dyed raffia, or grass, fringe covers the shoulders of the masker.

The Maskmaker

Maskmakers in the Congo hold an important leadership position. Each mask has an important story or meaning that must be learned by the artisan. These maskmakers are not trying to make a "work of art." Instead, their goal is to create the right image for the spirit that each mask represents. That image has been handed down through generations of maskmakers. A maskmaker may not know how or why a mask first came into being. Even so, the original mask design is still used as the model for masks made today.

A young maskmaker learns his craft in secret from an older maskmaker in the village. The power of the mask must be handled with great care and skill. Maskmakers believe that even the wood used to make a mask contains a powerful spirit that must be treated correctly. The maskmaking tools are also treated with great care. Tree-cutting and carving are all done according to rules that have been passed down.

Forming and Decorating the Mask

These maskmakers use decorations and colors that carry on their tribe's traditions. Grasses, leaves, and bark are used to cover the head, neck, and even the masker's body. Animal materials, such as feathers, ivory, and bone, are added for decoration. Even the colors of the mask are a part of the tradition of each tribal group. Popular colors are black, red, and white. The shape of the mask changes, depending on the tribe's tradition and whether it is a human or animal form. Masks can be flat or shaped like a bell, heart, bird, or animal. The animal shapes chosen may differ, depending on the wildlife in a tribe's area.

▲ Young maskmakers and dancers learn from older village maskers and priests. They pass on tribal secrets that bring special powers to the mask and to the masked dancer.

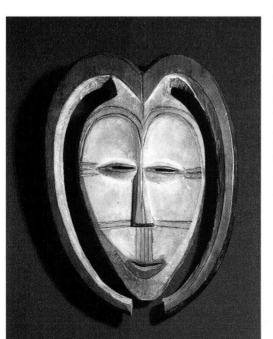

◄ Some masks are shaped in the form of animals. This mask is in the shape of a ram, a symbol of power.

40

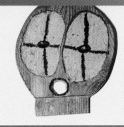

Tools

- pencil
- C-clamps
- towel
- wood chisels, 1/4-in. and 1/2-in. wide (.5 and 1 cm)
- wooden or rubber mallet, a special kind of hammer
- wood rasp or file
- paintbrushes

Materials

- 3/4-in. (2 cm) cedar or pine boards
- paper
- small chunk of clay
- carpenter's wood glue
- sandpaper
- acrylic paints
- beeswax furniture polish
- shells, beads, leather, metal, or fabric (optional)
- picture hanger

Design and carve a wooden mask that represents your own life experiences.

Experiment with Woodcarving

Before you begin, learn a few useful techniques. Practice on a scrap of the wood you will use for your mask. Carve and shape the scrap until you feel comfortable with the tools. Test different sizes of chisels. **Follow the important safety guidelines.**

V-cut

1. Practice making a V-cut. Draw two parallel lines about 1/2-inch (1 cm) apart. Shade in the area between the lines that will be carved away. Draw a cutting line down the center. *(See diagram.)*

2. Clamp the scrap wood tightly to a solid table. Protect the table with an old towel.

3. Make stop-cuts all along the cutting line. To make this cut, grasp a chisel firmly by the handle. Hold it straight up and down, with the cutting edge on the cutting line. Tap the chisel with the mallet hard enough to cut well into the board. Make all stop-cuts the same depth. *(See diagram.)*

4. Finish the V-cut. Place the chisel on one of the outside lines. Turn the slanted edge of the chisel upward. Make a slanting cut from the outside line to the bottom of the stop-cuts. Make another slanting cut from the other side to create a V-shaped trench. *(See diagram.)*

Woodcarving Safety

- **Have an adult work with you.**

- Learn the correct way to use a tool, and use it for its intended purpose only.

- Always clamp the wood to a firm base before carving. Protect the table with an old towel.

- Use common sense! Never put your fingers in front of the chisel when you are carving. Cut away from yourself and others.

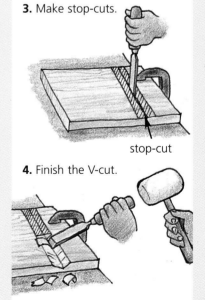

3. Make stop-cuts.

stop-cut

4. Finish the V-cut.

V-cut

1. Practice a V-cut.

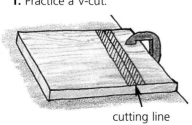

cutting line

Straight-Edged Shape

1. Experiment with carving a straight-edged shape. Draw a simple shape on the scrap wood with a pencil or pen. Shade in the waste area – the area that will be carved away. Turn the slanted side of the chisel toward the waste. Make stop-cuts all along the cutting line. *(See diagram.)*

2. Use a wedge-cut to remove the wood in the waste area. To make this cut, hold the chisel at a low angle. Turn the slanted edge of the chisel up. Aim the chisel toward the stop-cuts. Tap the chisel gently with the mallet to wedge up a sliver of wood. Try to carve in the same general direction as the grain of the wood. *(See diagram.)*

3. Carve all the way around the shape as deep as your stop-cuts. Work slowly, one thin layer at a time. If a thick chunk is wedged up, you are probably holding the chisel too high.

Rounded Shape

1. Not all the shapes on a mask will have straight edges. Practice rounding the edges. Draw a shape as before. Make stop-cuts, and remove the waste. Then use a small chisel to round the edges of the shape. *(See diagram.)*

2. The outside edges of the mask will probably also be rounded. Draw a line on the top surface to show the high point of the curve. Draw a cross section on each side of the board, as shown. Shade the waste area. *(See diagram.)*

3. Use a wedge-cut to remove the wood in the waste area little by little. Check the cross section to make sure you are carving a smooth, rounded edge and not an angle. *(See diagram.)*

◄ Round the outside edges of the scrap of wood.

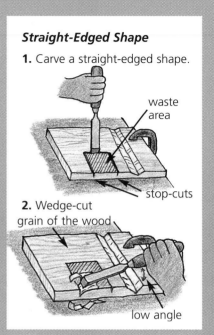

Straight-Edged Shape

1. Carve a straight-edged shape.

waste area

stop-cuts

2. Wedge-cut

grain of the wood

low angle

Rounded Shape

1. Round the edges.

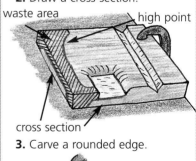

2. Draw a cross-section.

waste area

high point

cross section

3. Carve a rounded edge.

Mask Hints

■ In the Congo, the mask is often a symbol of a spirit-being, such as the earth or the wilderness.

■ Masks are carved with faces that look like humans or animals, but the features are enlarged and simplified.

■ Masks often combine the eyes, horns, noses, and beaks of several different animals. This is so the mask wearer can receive the power of all those animals.

■ Mask faces are almost always symmetrical, or balanced.

Plan Your Mask

3. Plan how you will finish your mask.

4. Make a clay model.

5. Draw a pattern.

Plan Your Mask

Carving a mask takes time and effort. Plan carefully before you begin to carve. Look at pictures of masks from the Congo for ideas. Read the Mask Hints at the left.

1. Decide what your mask will represent. Choose something that is meaningful to you from your own experience. For example, your mask could portray the spirit of a river, mountain, or city. It could be a symbol of peace, freedom, or creative energy.

2. Make several small drawings of the mask face. What human or animal characteristics will you include in your mask? How will the facial features relate to the idea you chose? Use each part of the face to show the spirit of your mask.

3. Plan how you will finish your mask. Masks in the Congo are decorated with shells, beads, buttons, bits of metal, and leather. You might like to add raffia, a grasslike fiber sold in craft stores, for hair or a beard. You can attach cloth horns or teeth cut from aluminum. You can also paint the mask face with lines, dots, and patterns. Be inventive! Anything that fits the character of your mask is acceptable. *(See diagram.)*

4. It is helpful to make a small clay model of your mask. Flatten out a little chunk of clay. Cut the outside shape of the mask. Form the highs and lows of each facial feature. Decide whether or not you will make holes for the eyes and mouth. *(See diagram.)*

5. When you have a clear idea of your mask, draw a pattern to the size you want. Draw the outside shape of the mask. Draw the eyes, mouth, nose, and other important features. Make shapes that you think you can carve easily. Shade in the waste areas. *(See diagram.)*

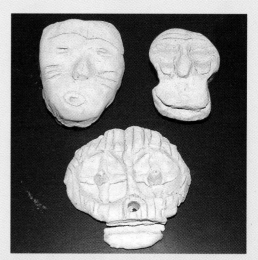

Use a small clay model ▶ to plan your mask.

Prepare the Wood

1. Decide on the thickness of your mask. It does not have to be very thick. Many Congolese masks are carved from flat planks of wood, only slightly rounded. However, you can glue two or more boards together for extra thickness. You can also glue a small piece of wood in one area. This is a good choice if one small part, like the nose, stands above the rest. *(See diagram.)*

2. Look your wood over carefully. Make sure there are no knotholes or splits. It is usually best if the grain runs from the top to the bottom of the mask. The ears, horns, and other narrow parts that extend out should have the grain running vertically. This will give them greater strength. *(See diagram.)*

3. Measure the wood. **Have an adult cut it to the right length for you.** If you plan to glue two sections, use boards that are flat. Make sure that they fit together snugly. Do not sand them, because the dust will make it hard for the glue to stick. Spread carpenter's wood glue on both surfaces. Put the boards together. Clamp them overnight with two C-clamps.

4. Cut out the paper pattern. Tape it on the wood, and trace around the outside. **Ask an adult to cut out the rough shape of the mask for you.** File the rough edges with a rasp or file. *(See diagram.)*

5. Tape the pattern onto the wood again. Trace over the cutting lines, pushing hard enough to leave a dent in the wood. Remove the pattern and redraw the lines with a pencil. Shade the waste areas. Draw the design clearly, so you don't carve away the wrong parts! *(See diagram.)*

6. Now glue small pieces of wood onto the mask, if you want. Stretch a small board over the piece and clamp on each side. *(See diagram.)*

◄ Remember to clamp your mask and carve safely.

Prepare the Wood

1. Decide on the thickness.

two boards

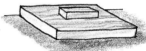

small piece glued

2. Examine the wood.

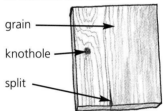

grain

knothole

split

4. Trace around the pattern.

5. Transfer the cutting lines to the wood.

6. Glue small pieces of wood.

Carve a Mask

1. Clamp the mask to a table with C-clamps. Slip a small scrap of thin wood between your mask and the clamp to protect the surface. Now you're ready to carve! *(Look at the photograph on page 44.)*

2. Begin by roughing out the general shape of the mask. Round the outside edges. Remove wood from the cheek area to make the nose stand out. Shape the eyes and mouth. Look at your clay model and drawings every now and then, to refresh your memory. If you aren't sure how to carve a shape, test it first on scrap wood. *(See diagram.)*

3. If you accidentally carve out more wood than you intended, don't worry! You can change your design, or you can glue the chip back in.

4. If you want to make holes for the eyes or mouth, **ask an adult to drill starter holes for you.** Then use a chisel to finish the shaping.

5. When most of the waste has been removed, begin to improve the facial features. You may need to redraw the cutting lines. Work slowly at this point. Use a narrow chisel to smooth the wood.

6. Sand the whole surface lightly with sandpaper. Wipe the surface down well to remove wood dust. Paint the mask with thinned acrylic paints if you want. **Protect your clothing with an old shirt or a smock. Remember, while acrylic paint is still wet, it can be removed with water. Once it dries, it cannot be removed.**

7. When the paint is dry, wipe the wood with several coats of beeswax furniture polish. Wax protects the wood from dirt and dust. Between coats, rub and polish your mask with a soft cloth to get a smooth shine.

8. Use wood glue to attach beads, raffia, or other materials to your mask. If you plan to hang your mask, attach a picture hanger to the back.

Carving Hints

■ Use a narrow chisel to stop-cut around curved areas, and a wide chisel for long straight areas.

■ If your chisels are dull, they will mash the wood rather than make a clean cut. **Ask an adult to sharpen your tools.**

Peaceful Cat, ▶
Mixed-Up Monkey,
and Bird Spirit masks
carved by students.

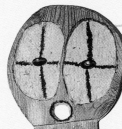

Glossary

animism the belief that everything in the world, including rocks, animals, and a thunderstorm, has a living spirit

anthropological relating to the study of the origin; behavior; and the physical, social, and cultural development of human beings

apartheid the South African system of racial segregation and political and economic discrimination

appliqué sewing technique where small pieces of fabric are cut out and sewn on top of each other

archaeological relating to the scientific study of past human life

artisans people who are skilled in an art, a craft, or a trade

deities gods

discrimination prejudiced, unfair treatment of a person based on his or her race, gender, or age, for example

embroidery decorative needlework

extinct no longer active or existing

hemisphere the northern and southern halves of the earth divided by the equator

literacy the ability to read and write; a skill that is needed in a country where people elect leaders and determine their own future

nomadic moving seasonally from place to place; having no fixed place of residence

plateau a level land surface raised sharply above land next to it on at least one side

rite of passage a ritual in a culture that marks a person's change from one stage of life to another

rituals a series of actions that are regularly followed, especially in a religious ceremony

sanctions penalties for a nation that does not respect the world view of human rights

savanna an open, grassy landscape with widely scattered trees

segregation the forced separation of a racial or ethnic group

symmetrical balanced or even

Abbreviation Key

sq.	square
mi.	miles
km	kilometers
ft.	feet
m	meters
in.	inches
cm	centimeters
F	Fahrenheit
C	Centigrade
g	grams

Resources

Kenya
Burch, Joann J. *Kenya–Africa's Tamed Wilderness.* Parsippany, NJ: Dillon, 1992
Coles, Janet, and Robert Budwig. *Beads: An Exploration of Bead Traditions Around the World.* New York: Simon & Schuster, 1997
Fisher, Angela. *Africa Adorned.* New York: Harry Abrams, 1984
LaDuke, Betty. *Africa: Through the Eyes of Women Artists.* Baltimore, MD: Africa World, 1991
Tomalin, Stefany. *Beads! Make Your Own Unique Jewelry.* London: David & Charles, 1988

Benin
Chambers, Catherine. *West African States: 15th Century to Colonial Era,* "Looking Back" series. Raintree Steck-Vaughn, 1999
Girshick Ben-Amos, Paula. *Art of Benin,* rev. ed. Washington, DC: Smithsonian, 1995
Koslow, Philip. *Benin–Lords of the River.* Broomall, PA: Chelsea House, 1996
Koslow, Philip. *Dahomey: The Warrior Kings,* "The Kingdoms of Africa" series. Broomall, PA: Chelsea House, 1996
Newman, Thelma. *Contemporary African Arts and Crafts: On-site Working with Art Forms and Processes.* New York: Crown, 1974
Sheehan, Sean. *Benin and Other African Kingdoms,* "Ancient Worlds" series. Austin, TX: Raintree Steck-Vaughn, 1999

South Africa

Bradley, Catherine. *The End of Aparteid,* "Causes and Consequences" series. Austin, TX: Raintree Steck-Vaughn, 1995

Flint, David. *South Africa,* "Modern Industrial World" series. Austin, TX: Raintree Steck-Vaughn, 1997

Maguire, Mary. *New Crafts: Wirework.* Chicago, IL: Lorenz Books, 1996

Pratt, Paula B. *The End of Apartheid in South Africa,* "Overview" series. San Diego, CA: Lucent, 1995

Shillington, Kevin. *Independence in Africa,* "Causes and Consequences" series. Raintree Steck-Vaughn, 1998

Congo

Adinoyi-ojo, Onukaba. *Mbuti,* "Heritage Library of African Peoples" series. New York, Rosen Group, 1995

Bridgewater, Alan, and Gill Bridgewater. *Carving Masks: Tribal, Ethnic & Folk Projects.* Pittsburgh, PA: Sterling, 1996

Lerner Geography Dept. Staff, ed. *Zaire in Pictures,* "Visual Geography" series. Minneapolis, MN: Lerner, 1992

Starr, Richard. *Woodworking With Kids.* Newton, CT: The Taunton Press, 1982

Stelzig, Christine. *Can You Spot the Leopard? African Masks.* Munich: Prestel-Verlag, 1997

Index

Acknowledgments

Special thanks to these students for their time and energy in making the project samples: Alden, Carrie B., Carrie S., Cassady, Kyle, Martina, and Sanya; and to Aisha, Arias, and Yemaya for their help. Thanks also to Kimeli Ole-Naiyomah; Patterson Family School, Eugene, Oregon; Barb Shirk; Stephen Reynolds; Diane Cissel, Terragraphics; Libris Solar; City Copy; Ruby Chasm; and Greater Goods. Special thanks to Casey Franklin for his patience and restraint. Thanks to the Eugene Public Library and the Salt Lake City Public Library reference librarians for their ongoing help.